Birthing Inadequacy

Parlour Press
15 Borealis Rd
High Level, AB
T0H 1Z0

www.tashtoo.com
Contact Information: tashahead@gmail.com

Birthing Inadequacy

COPYRIGHT 2014

First Edition, November 2014

ISBN: 978-1-312-57616-2

Cover Art by Kim Mosdell

"To quiet my mind is impossible. The duality of my inner selves a constant and clamouring white noise composed of degradation and limiting beliefs. My survival depends on finding that thing that speaks louder than my demons. That thing is poetry."

Natasha Head

There's no secret to writing poetry. An inspired thought, a nightmare, a dream, a wish. It is a simple recording of life, as it happens. A poet cannot find herself without a muse. I owe a great deal of credit for this collection of ponderings to a few, very special people.

PapaG...if not for your soundtrack, support and friendship, many of these pieces would not have come to pass. I think you'll know which ones.

Andrea, you provided strength and inspiration on days where I gave thought to simply tossing my pen. I will remain forever grateful.

My family, who have done their best to master dealing with the moods of a pen wielding, word addicted fiend who insists there's poetry in every act, be it of love, hate or indifference.

And of course, my daughter Lauren, who's spirit, kindness and heart make me realize, we might not be so inadequate after all...stay you!

Power to the Poets

~N

Table of Contents

In My Dark
At My Alter
Home
Wolf Born
Fault Lines
An Ode to Fairy Godmothers
Alabaster Disaster
Sink

Third Trimester
Fire in the Sky
Decisions
Amber
Panic
Stray
Rats
Tigress
Thru Infinity
A Celebration Song
Backbone
I Wonder
Not an Option
Too Easy to Love
Frailty
Put This to Memory
She Will Not Mourn
How High a Cost
Rape Culture
Thrill Alone

AfterBirth

Conception

The Garden

Would we have written history differently,
If we could have reached the shore first?
Swimming from the blackest depths of our beginning,
Where we knew not separation?

Who decided it would be your rib
That would represent our birth?
Who claimed us as token companionship,
Temptress?
Going against the very science of creation?

Because you stepped to shore
Lacking womb
Perhaps it was not the fire in your loins
That placed us on a lower rung...

Rather a deep seated resentment
In not having the ability to lend life
To your legacy
Without our bodies.

Would it have been different
If we were to have taken our fists
Ripping open your chest with our very hands
Laying claim to a part of you?

Perhaps even then you knew our weakness,
Knowing we would let you write the story
For we were born from your body
To please.

Was it your voice that whispered
Through the belly of the snake
Who had his way
With our desires?

Like the vehicles for mistrust
You painted us
We have always done your bidding.

Was it you who decided
Where we would place the fig leaf
Who painted our nakedness
In lust and hell fire?

Was this the first attack
Against our nurturing ways
That would see us battling
For centuries?

Fighting amongst ourselves
Petty and indifferent
Seeing our sister's bodies burn
For dancing with the devil of your making?

It is the soil that births creation
But it is the hearts of man
Where evil is born.

In your lust for power
In your inability to see value
Beyond leaving your mark
It is at your hand we've been branded.

Do you think, perhaps
Our world would have evolved differently
If we had stood as equals
Lending the balance

She's been craving?
Do you ever wonder, what's missing?
Our garden, now a sea of digital vegetation
Where mothers are finding voices

Where confidence has ripened
And courage is fostered.
The quality of the seed
Determines the value of the crop

If Mother Nature
Blesses you with the climate
To harvest.

Are you prepared now,
To place proper value upon the womb
Where your future is housed?

Are you prepared
To look beyond to what our world
Should have been?
Was she was always meant to be?
What came first?
The seed, or the womb?
One without the other
Does not a fertile garden make.

Motherless

She stands upon the shore, toes buried in the cool sand
Even the cry of the gulls cannot penetrate her walls,
Nor does the sea foam of the incoming tide warrant her
attention.

The sun is setting, a ball of molten fire in the sky
Melting into the ruddiness of the burnt umber water
That is the Bay of Fundy.

There are ships upon the horizon now
Returning home from their pirating adventures
Traps set, quotas met, yet she pays no mind.

She has stood like this for many life times
Held in place, enchanted, by the lure of the sea
The taker, the maker, the gut of humanity

But it has been in this life time, she has watched her
bleed out
As her children wash up upon the shore
Slick, greasy, awash in rainbow black,

Poisoned at the hands of her stewards
Whose minds she has witnessed slowly invaded
Corrupted by nothing less than the desire for more.

The salt of the sea must not be mistaken
For the salt that now stings her parted lips.
Swallowing tear drops, born of the mutilation of all that
was once pure.

Her heart is now the heaviest it has ever been, her blood
The blood of generations, faltering in its power
As it tries to fuel a heart that has lost hope.

A sand crab skitters before her, knowing better than to approach
There is a wildness in her eyes, a fire that smoulders
Despite the air of defeat that surrounds her.

That her children were born of free will
That she will guide only when asked.
Who knew the world would fall under the pressure of freedom.

The time for influence and guidance is now long past.
The children, who, in her efforts to let them live
Have somehow forgotten her...her love, her nurturing, her wrath

They have grown wild in their lack of supervision
The few have chosen the fate of many
And now the cleansing will come.

Between slim and delicate fingers
A simple clam shell, long abandoned
Catches the glow of the sun's last rays

And with a sigh that stops the waves
She tosses it gently to the water's edge
And for the first time

Mother turns from tide
Knowing the time has come
To let the fate of her children, run its course.

First Trimester

The Test

Blown out bulbs lend an eerie glow to her surroundings.
They were never good at maintenance.
Honestly, never really cared.
Will all that change now?

A white stick, two pink lines...
Something she never dreamed she would be able to accomplish
Glowing hot pink in this surreal glow of doom.
The fear of inadequacy silenced for now,
She has proven her worth...to a point.

All the arguments over the years.
Sacrificing long held beliefs in exchange for diamonds and gold.
Pomp and ceremony,
Celebration...

Now she realizes what for.
The easy agreement.

She doesn't want to tell.
She doesn't want to admit she never wanted it as bad.
All the memories of suffering,
All the current events as the world around her crumbles.

What has she done?
What innocence will she be responsible for destroying?
Would they understand if she told them...
That fear is the shine in her eyes, not the joy they assume.

The dim lighting gives rise to shadows,
The pink, burning in her hand.
Flowers dance on cheap wall paper
Mildew in ancient grout attacks her sense of smell.

Aware she is falling back, aware she is falling down.
Back against barker board tile,
Sliding and tearing against her skin,
Memories of what she has lived through assault her

Without mercy,
Stealing her breath,
Forcing her to realize
The white pain of fear
She is responsible.
She is creator.

She will be mother.

Lord help the innocence birthed at her hands.

Blue Bicycle

Though she was desperate for a banana seat and streamers on the handle bars,
she could not hide the pride that came with her first, official two-wheeler.

Black grips, black leather seat, and flashy, blue chrome paint. She can remember how two red bands sparkled round its cross bar.

She was a girl surrounded by boys, and she could hold her own. Neighbors and their cousins fought to keep up as she spun out on the gravel driveway, kicking up stones and dust in their faces.

That bike transported her to every world she wanted to visit. To the grocer on the corner who carried only the freshest mud for her pies. To the fishing hole down around the block where they could swim with Jaws and survive. Holly Hobby may have been the rage, but she was Daisy Duke outrunning J.R across the Dallas Plains in the General Lee.

That bike also taught her, her first hard lesson.

On the morning she woke and found it had been taken from the side wall where she would lean it up with care, every night when they were finally called in to supper.

She cried. Over and Over, she wailed. It was her first loss. It was the first time she remembered thinking maybe just because they called you friend, didn't really mean they were.

It was the birth of doubt in a five year old mind.

And it was only the beginning.

Sunday Morning (circa 1979)

The kitten was lying at the end of the driveway, head on the asphalt, tail on the gravel, as though sneaking some warmth from the heat of the early morning sun.

It was early, quiet, the grownups still sleeping, soon to rise with heavy heads from the night before, where Kenny Rogers and Johnny Cash had dueled into the wee hours of dawn. She knew one was going to end up in Folsem Prison for gambling.

Outside, she was alone. She was afraid for the kitten, her newest pet. He must have been as tired as the grownups, out all night, hunting mice.

A morning of Sunday School awaited. A chance to show off their goodness. She had even, for the first time ever, managed to memorize her scripture. She knew God would be proud.

Her neighbor would be transporting her to the church that morning, along with her three sons. She was a loud woman with a cackle of a laugh that made the girl think of the witch in Snow White. Disney was her Sunday evening ritual.

As she climbed into the back seat of the car, she explained how carefully Blackie was resting. How he must have been so tired from his late night. She asks the cackling neighbor to please be careful not to wake him.

The woman stares at the five year old, lost in the lumbering back seat of a station wagon, her steal blue gaze in that rear-view mirror boring its way into the memory of a little girl.

The little girl knows she will never be able to forget how that cackle turned to evil, cruel, as the laughing woman ran over the cat and bounced them onto the pavement on route to the church for their weekly dose of forgiveness.

That cat was gone when they returned. Her oldest boy harassed the little girl for weeks over its death.

It was cruelty for the simple purpose of being cruel.

A lesson that should never have to be learned.

Friendless

A little girl,
Dressed in her finest,
Stands alone against the brick wall
Children surround her,
But none reach out.

Her Charlie Brown lunchbox
Bangs against her belly
As she watches them play,
Friends from before.

She is happy to watch,
Content.

Years later
She will have no memory
Of this day.

Still, it will find itself implanted
Through the voice of a mother
Who speaks of fear and tears,

Driving by the school yard
To see if she can see her little one.
She learns that friends are important.

She learns that if she can have enough
They won't pay as close attention.

She makes it her mission.
She doesn't want her mom to cry.

Bully

The day was cold.
A chubby little girl
Forces with all her might
Snow pants over a round belly
Anxious to get outside

Cheeks rosy
Pinched and poked
Proud of the baby fat
They tell her not to worry about

Waddling to the playground
A silver, shining strip
Of the most perfect ice
Delivered overnight

Jack Frost was busy

She takes her place in line
The boy in front
Tickling her chin with the top of his toque
No bigger than a blackfly

"Hey Fatso...you'll crack the ice"

He is smiling like a devil
Turns hastily
And runs with all his might.

He glides smoothly to the end
Never stumbling

She stands in near tears
Knowing it's not yet her time to slide

If there's a god in heaven
He'll forgive her
She need not be concerned with grace.

Her cheeks no longer rosy from the cold
She feels the heat of hatred burning inside her.

The others in the line have caught on.
Fatso's gonna slide

She watches the graceful one at the end
Proud, pompous,
Her mother would call him a little shit
But she's not allowed to talk like that

Fatso runs with all her might
A plumb bullet

Barreling for all she's worth
Towards the still dancing boy
So caught up in his perfection
He doesn't see her coming

He flies through the air on impact
Landing so hard on his rump
His front teeth bust through his lip
His head bounces off the ice

The tears deplete his pride
He faints at the sight of the blood

Accidents happen
Explains the lunch monitor.

She never hears "Fatso" again.
Kids can be so cruel.

Confirmation

The waiting room is a sickly green.
The breakfast she woke ravenous for
Sits like a lead weight in her stomach.

She was never a breakfast eater.
The child obviously is.

The cup she holds in her hand is warm,
Frightfully unnecessary
Yet protocol insists
She degrades herself.

The others look from the cup
To her
And back again.

She smiles, shrugs
It what she was trained to do.

They are coughing, hacking, bleeding, sweating
None of this can be good for new life
Inhaled through the body of the host.
Still, this is protocol.

A ten-thirty appointment is honored an hour late
The child is hungry again.
Never more conscious of the fact
She is no longer living for self,

The host grows fearful.

What secrets will be revealed
As she climbs aboard the magic alter
Slipping into silvered stirrups
To display the biggest source of her shame?

Instruments, cold hands, gelatinous lotions
Small talk of the most awkward nature
Pushed, prodded, exposed in ways she has never been

No mention of anything more
Than once confirmation is received
The bloodletting will begin

The shredding of her dignity
To be continued.

***

She hurries home
To their cute little house
On the cute little lot.

She makes no mention of shame
As she lets the doctor's "unofficial" diagnosis
Escape from her lips.

He is ecstatic.
This is what he has been waiting for.
This is what they've been working toward.

A perfect family
In a perfect house.

She can tell now,
His relief obvious.
His concern, never before spoken of

Never to be spoken of
Underlying the weight of the conversation.
They are normal after all.

The census office
Breathes a sigh of relief
As two more victims
Step willingly toward the dream.

Easier to count.
Easier to control.
It's not just about them anymore.

May their families rejoice.
Long live the picket fences.

Little Pieces ~ Little Hopes

Each little piece
dancing before me
out of place, rearranged,
spinning
like so many faceted tear drops
catching the rays of the sun
that never breaks through to shine on my heart

I feel...with every ounce of my being
every pain shared
is it any wonder I've been left fragmented

the sick
the hungry
the dying

taking up so much space
where is the room for love
when atrocities of our own making
weight down our soul

Shift now
consciousness distorted
a chemical cocktail
to stop the spinning

winning?

It was never about winning
I could care less where the pieces fit

as long as they fit...

I could care less how fast they get put back together
as long as I can cling to the faith that it will happen...

Broken...perhaps
fixable...maybe
Lovable?
Christ...I hope so.

They told me that's why I'm here....

To love
to be loved

They told me that's why we're all here

and that makes me wonder
if THEY weren't like the others

telling me what I want to hear
in hopes I'll join the army
march with the masses
and forget the truth
I was born with.

Broken...perhaps
fixable...of course
lovable?

More than this world can handle.

Anything Boys Can Do, Girls Can Do Better

A mantra that was mandatory
Surrounded by the vile beasts as I was.

I'll never forget the cackling neighbor
Propping two of her naked offspring
Into my Fred Flintstone wading pool.

It was a lesson in the male anatomy
No child should have ever been subjected to.

How I fought to prove this.
Over and Over.

No girl softball league?
No worries.
I'll just play with the boys.

No one ever noticed I was scared to death.
I never copped to the teasing
I just played harder.

The basketball teams
The soccer fields
The street hockey on lunch break.

Competition ran a fire in my blood.
Elbows and pushing
As hard as you could get away with.

Losing sucked.
It showed on the face of every parent

Who screamed from the bleachers

Desperate for a retirement income
A golden dream.

I gave up on mine,
The year I broke the arm of a frail little lady
(see what I did there)
Who never should have been on the field.

If you don't know the rules
You shouldn't play the game.
It felt good to push her into the goal post
To hear the crack
To see her cry.

It was the first time I scared myself.
It was the first time I realized

We've all got it wrong.

The cheering parents
Showed the true faces of the monsters they were

The win
For the first time
Sour

The first sleepless night due to guilt.
Undeserved accolades
An innocent injured
I was 11 years old.

Look Me in the Eye and Tell Me That

We learn very young this art of lying.
What it takes to make a person believe you.
In my house, it was eye to eye.
Full frontal contact.
If you couldn't pull it off...
Your fate was sealed.

It was rare I would use this art form to my advantage.
Never with Mom and Dad.
It simply couldn't be done.
Guilt was a lesson I learned young too.

Never with someone I cared about,
They deserve more of me than that.
You can't build a relationship on lies,
No matter how bright and white they may be.

But when it came to being looked down upon?
When it came to adults who got off on power tripping
over children?
I was a devil.

Grade six brought me the "strictest" teacher I would
ever have.
Steel grey eyes that could burn a hole in your head.
She never lost a shootout with those blazing bullets.
She was proud of this.
It was legend.

I destroyed it.
From across the room.

The most insignificant failing.
So miniscule, I can't even remember the indiscretion.
But that day was my day to take the bullet.

I took it
No backing down.
Denied the indiscretion
With my own steel.
Six rows of desks separated us
I was frozen in my place
Scared to death
But still staring

Eye to eye,
The classroom silenced around us.

Perhaps she realized how foolish she must have looked
Perhaps there was no real joy in terrifying children after
all...

I should have been so lucky.
She broke the contact
Dropped her gaze

Turning on her heel
She whipped open the door
A deathly white, slender finger
Pointed into the darkened hall.

I left the room
My head held high.
I may have spent the afternoon
Alone and in a hallway corner

But that afternoon was golden.

I learned even adult bullies
Could be defeated.

Suicide Watch

They expect me to be wallowing
broken and battered
blaming myself for life not having met with my
expectations
They have never once questioned what those
expectations were,
so, if we're being truthful, it's their own expectations for
me
that gives cause for concern.

It's suicide watch on the down-low
Assumptions made based on my latest, random doodle
Ink blot mentality leaves little room for my voice
not that they'd listen anyway
They know best...they always have.

The lack of tears, of course, means there is misdirected
fault
No skin off my back
I've been apologizing for the last thirty years
Accepting of the blame
in hopes of shutting them up.

Every dream I have ever sacrificed in my sick and
twisted hunt for approval
Lies weighted at my feet in a mockery of ball and chain
Shackles I no longer accept responsibility for
finally finding the courage to beg release.

Would they feel better, I wonder
If I were to take this blade

and prove my addiction to attention

Just a sliver, not too deep
enough for them to feel needed, important, right
Take my medicine
cry like I'm supposed to
and never once tell them
I'm not scared anymore.

Waxing Wisdom

If I choose to use this magic
to help you balance invisible scales
can you guarantee
the perception of your counter weight
has not been altered.

She watches all you know
waxing, waning
controlling the pull of the tides
and all who walked erect from her sea

I'll believe your story
but it is her decision to remove your veil.

Eyes wide and awake
caught in the glare of her silver crescent
are you prepared to believe?

How many rituals
How many idols
before you realize
her magic is born in you?

Will you shout it to the heavens
upon this revelation of her truth?

Will your mighty ego rise
swallowing the spirit we worked so hard to reveal.

Can you know your power
without coming to abuse it.

The universal law of three

It comes back you know, always
be it white, black, gray

It always has
throughout every shift in thinking
every movement in culture
She has witnessed all

and in her all knowing
the scales cannot help
but balance

Dark Matter

Slipstream
particles collide
transference

Realities merge
coupling
sensing the potential

Is this the me you wish to see
Propped up pedestal
trip the switch

Blackness now as you ponder
In the dark there is no sense of my self
which might influence your desire

Shortcut now
space and time need pay no mind
the wormhole trumps their power

Now meek and mild
no more girl gone wild
you knew that taste would sour

Pulsing waves distort my senses
while you decide
where you'll mark your fences

Collar tight, the leash is snug
have you determined
this is love?

Born

Did my shadow darken your doorway
as you slept with one eye open?
Your little brain, pitter-pattering its way
through to dawn
when relief comes in having to face
only what you can see.

Sleeping below a rainbow
serves only those who refuse to dance
to the joy of the spectrum
the beat of a different realm.

You've paused so long at yesterday
the roots now ensnare my feet.
Straight up always
put prone to changing minds

My god wears a coat of many colors
to hide her perfect form.
It only goes to prove
in her image I have failed.

Goodness bleeds as does the bad
but its flow is smoother
allowing me to sleep at night...
provided my imagination agrees to not run away
for it is my dictator
and I am prone to fancy.

I've been told countless times
I've outgrown the need for fairies

yet I refuse to accept conditions
acceptable to most.

Therefore
doomed to swim in rainbow rain
I face most my storms alone
for I've not the words
nor the magic
to make the blind see.

Mourning Glory

There is a core to the blackness
a throbbing heart that pulses
to unheard rhythms of despair...
Layer after layer
the light is buried deep

Days spent in flannel pajamas
housebound
staring over a garden
where the flowers cease to bloom

They judge
Demand action
as though there is control over the blackness
as though somehow with your rising
the flowers will once again blossom.

In the blackness there is truth
that all we do, all we feel
every single tear we cry
matters not to the core
for its fertility trumps time and space
It was before
It is now
It will always be.

A spirit lingers here
that fell from the sky without warning
Like a magnet
tethered to the heart of blackness
it is attached.

It was before
It is now
It will always be.

The truth of my faith is blackness
for in it
there is no light
to ignite my illusion.

The headstone
far enough away
I can pretend it's not even there.

Warrior Vs. Soldier

If you could take it back...would you?
So often, actions are nothing more than response to
stimuli...
Words from the heart
acts out of anger
rage through terror.
No matter the device
the constant instigator
Shit disturber

Like the rubber band, stretching, cracking
I finally split
Propelled beyond your wildest imagination
Mutation
Flesh shredded,
as the beast you never knew I owned
emerges.

Tearing apart the very being they had you convinced I
was.
Swallow now
Once breathing returns to normal.
No fear, my dear
Blood shed is common when one awakens to truth.
It seems to be the nasty way of our species

Killing to hang on to a 17th century rule book
Based on a playing field that was eroded by the time
It made it to mass publication.
Where are we to hang the noose
When there are only brambles and castrated clay?

The sea swallowed the tree eons ago.

You whisper such sweet words
When your survival is on the line...
Yet once my back is turned
You can't resist throwing the knife...
It's the way of the soldier...
To do the bidding of others.

While the free thinking warriors
Take the bullets
For those too afraid to speak
It is what it is
It was what it was
And I am nothing
If not free.

If you could take it back
I wouldn't let you
I don't shed skin...for just anyone.

Gestation

Ripped from the very skin that birthed me
ego fractured, tattered, not much matters
when this state of being becomes existence

Ribbons of flesh permeated
dyed, reviled, but never reconciled
as anything more than dead space

mutated, petri dish concoction
festering on window sill, complacency had had its fill
Here is where the sunshine goes to die

Black matter, mad hatter
Alice was never wanted here
wrapped in a bottle-blonde psychosis...You know this!

Anti-poster child
getting me all riled
up...
Dare I give a fuck?

When it's all I've left to give?

Loose change slipped from my pocket long ago
A feast for those who've not known bread
better off fed?

I see the army that marches has grown in number
while I've been content to slumber
Who knew white rabbit...could be so cruel.

A Pound of Flesh

Should one desire a pound of flesh
to balance one's scales of worth
allow me to caution you...

The vessel which houses
you, our eternal beings of light
is proportionally designed
so that shelter from the shadows
can be obtained.

I am left but to question
should that pound of flesh be delivered
at the hands of one who knows not the map
Shelter may well be revoked
based on a technicality found
within the word of the law.

Again, I must caution
should you choose to uphold said word
please do not look down upon this vessel
for the eternal being of light which resides within
learned long ago that "legal" and "moral" are not
found on the same page, no matter
what hand of god has held office
or bought the pound of flesh
from the rump who happens to reside upon the bench.

To truly balance the scales
there is no need for the delivery of any amount of flesh
simply perhaps
the hand of god who holds present office

should find within himself
the courage to offer to his people
all of his flesh
in the form of new laws
based not on an economy driven agenda

rather
based upon a desire to build a better world

Should the hand of present god
not know within his heart
what is needed

(ie: compassion, empathy, understanding, love)

then, and only then
should we let our flesh fall upon the steps
of every grand and pompous house of the lord
For it is we
who in our silence
at the hands of our apathy
have allowed the lord his manor.

Pine Box

Shadows, gray dust settling
silhouettes dancing
though the symphony is silent

Sunbeams know not of the darkness
for the veil lies heavy
crushed velvet, scent of ancestors

ghosts cry from behind the curtain.
Beckoning, luring
bloodline, entanglement

The long white box
carelessly perched upon the cement
where headstones topple

It's perfume is the scent of decay
despite the newness of its package
and the petals turn to dust

left to be blown to the cosmos
on the breath of the forgotten
T'was not the wind

that caressed your cheek.
Mythic battles of conquered hearts
broken, bruised

left to die
as lungs grow blacker
ensnared now

by dreams never to be forgotten
as they march on through eternity
and dance upon the graves.

Trouble the Struggle

Struggle
We cling to it
as though we're not living
unless we are...

Struggling.

We covet things
stupid stuff
when we are told we can't have.

Like spoiled children
we grow determined to find a way
no matter the cost

No matter the consequences.
Who are you to tell me what should be?
I'll prove you wrong

but who laughs last?

They call us a free society
yet we are content to be chained by paper.
Who needs shackles

When the people follow willingly
tied to the land
that was never meant to be owned

Let alone divided.

Fences don't keep the enemy out
They keeps us in
where we can be counted
valued
stamped
and approved

Then done away with
like fish in a barrel
if we dare stand against
the system
and lie about our worth

Trans Union
Equifax
Keeping score
Keeping track
Not a chance to take one back
when you're a simple number
and they're ready to attack.

Second Trimester

Ultrasound

She is blonde, tiny...and sneering at her.
She is evil.
The young mother-to-be can see it,
In the cold, steel blue of her icy eyes.
This "nurse" is not happy here.

Stuck in a room
Filled to overflowing
With the promise of life.

Growing, expectant mothers
Should bring joy to her face,
But the young woman now realizes
The world cares not for her joy.

***

The nurse's tiny hands are rough,
Bony...freezing
As abusive as the gun metal gaze.
She is barking orders
Demanding subservience
Against a tissue paper backdrop.
The young mother is meek, mild
Convinced this must be the norm.
Scared to death,
And close to tears.

***

The young mother-to-be is alone
Waiting on the inside.
Her love,

As scares and as new to this as her,
Paces the hallway on the outside.
The room is shuttered, dark
Pepto-Bismol pink
As though making fun of good cheer.
Beeps, like gunshots in the silence
Echo off the walls
A weak and dying sun
Filters through the blind
Watered down and useless.
Her breath is labored
Her pulse racing
She fights to remember protocol
Drill sergeant commands.
She is worried she will disappoint him.
Not ask all the right questions.
Not be able to give any answers.
She is close to panic,
The small quiet voice in her head grows louder
Echoing
Over and over
"What the hell have you done?"

***

He enters briskly, his face stern.
Is this the one she has been waiting for?
The door slams.
He takes the chair beside her.
No words are spoken.
There is pressure,
cold, slippery
as he pushes the strange instrument
against her tender flesh.

She is stunned,
silent,
violated,
fighting the tears that have been threatening
since the beginning of her surreal journey.
Images appear on the monitor.
Faint, pixilated…
liquidy.
The man remains quiet,
making notes with a firm hand
on an ancient and discolored clipboard.
His other hands continues to push,
to hurt.
A sudden halt,
and he is gone.
She is left, once again, alone
for what seems like an eternity,
the sickly, pink walls
closing in.

***

The wicked witch returns.
She orders the young woman to clean herself up.
"But I don't know"
She is ashamed at the pathetic weakness in her voice.
Soft, breaking.
"I told you to ask the doctor if you wanted to know!"
The nurse is pure venom.
In her exasperated sigh
the young woman hears the chorus of voices
of every one she has ever disappointed.
She can't go back not knowing.
This was the news he would be waiting to hear.

For once...she can't let it go.
It can't start like every other thing she has ever attempted.
She couldn't mess this up so soon.
"What Doctor"
Certainly the nurse couldn't mean
the unspeaking brute
with the cold hands
who she had so obviously interrupted.
The wicked witch throws the towel aside
in a childish tantrum
and storms from the room.
The young woman stands her ground.
She will not leave without her answer.
The nurse and the brute,
return.

***

His voice is as rough and as cold as his hands.
He brings the screen back to life.
Green blips as the image rebirths.
Black and white.
Date and time.
The young woman's name
dancing across the top.
The nurse stands at attention in the corner.
Eyes all the while glaring at the young woman.
She has finally given in to the tears,
no longer caring.
She is seeing for the first time.
Knowing now,
beyond any doubt

everything intuition has already told her.
A little girl,
head, toes, fingers, nose,
who needs to somehow make it in this world.
She will not let the overworked practitioners
steal from this moment.
She will not let them fill her with shame,
nor guilt.
She hones in on the tiny image.
The vision of her growing,
healthy,
daughter.
The weight of the responsibility,
unlike anything she could ever imagine.

The Forgotten One

Who would think the better half could so easily be forgotten.
Written out of our history
Consumed by the seed of the holy ghost
though no crown or title would she wear.

Who would think our "god"
in whose image we were made
would share in our carnal desires
when rule states heavenly bodies
should be consumed one at a time

unless you listen to the other son
who allows his boys a few more toys

And so I was left to smolder
when water boarding wouldn't work
Connected to earth, to tide, to love
that you chose to name as devil

For centuries it seems
I have been tied to your flames
Waving undergarments on fire
Asking you to do the math...

To have one without the other...
and you regard your world with confusion?
An unbalanced scale will tilt to the heaviest side
there is no magic formula here

We were left outside when the ladder to heaven was built
back doored by the popular vote
Our magick was decidedly evil
Our bodies, the most toxic elixir
Though it was a poison born in the minds of men.

And while I remain flattered at the strength of their stake
flames licking at my toes for eons
I have watched us regain our footing
only to slip in our efforts to become like them
and I watch those scales tip further

Yin and Yang
Ebb and flow
Strength and love
Your human army falters
as universal laws predict your failings
you, content to turn away
resisting the one change that would right every wrong

You are no better
You are no worse
Your designs and labels
created to feed the ego that now governs
will be your undoing.

All good people know
as long as there is inequality
there will be war
there will be famine
there will be unnecessary deaths in untold numbers

I urge you now to wake
To face the errors of your ways
This is not the voice of the father you pray to
simply the hope of the mother
you have forgotten

Thoughtless

Without faith in yourself
how can you proclaim faith in the unknown

Children bow to elders
seeking wisdom of the ages

Systemized and trained
brainwashed to think they know

It is the elders who pass the poison
in knockoff kool-aid cups.

Text book programming
vibration through brand name sponsors

as the parasite seeks out host
latching on, the sucking begins

dumbing down, dumbing down, dumbing down

Occasionally...a rift appears
when kool-aid seeps through unseen cracks

to meet with a mind immune
from teachers to preachers

stymied
The lab coat army marches to the rescue

Prescription pads
and medicare

We'll pay to ensure you meet current criteria
and should treatment prove ineffective

We'll pay to make sure all know
the failure you are destined to be

No purpose for society
medicated, hated

your free thinking mind
sacrilege
against pre programmed limitations.

Confession

Confessing to the choices made for the simple case of pleasing others, absolves me of my right to complain.

Confessing the fear behind the same choices means I can at least express my shame through words.

I always feared disappointing my parents. I love them so much. Know all they have sacrificed for me. Know well how hard they have worked, only to be ensnared in a system that takes away the shrinking hours of their lives. I write these words now, fearing that same disappointment. Different choices would have helped me keep them from this.

I was always afraid no one would love me. To this day, I cannot accept a compliment, let alone the love of a partner who thinks and speaks so highly of me...even when I'm not listening. This humble humility is a falsehood. I am not worthy.

I am terrified of raising a daughter in my shadow of self-doubt and loathing. I am scared to death my disease will be contracted, to be carried on. How many generations strong is the evil already?

How do I, one who cannot even face herself in the mirror, bring an end to this madness?

Wanting

A simple life was the only desire
Until her dreams were railroaded

Hijacked by the wanton ambitions
Of a world that would never recognize
the definition of enough.

How many hours wasted in vain?
Only to prove she could want more than she needed?

The sacrifice of hours never to be returned.
Days lost to an insatiable need
And the confusion of not knowing why.

The drive to prove worth to others
Through wanting
Achieving

The drive to prove worth to herself
Through losing
Letting go

...and running away

In My Dark

I took you home
When I realized you liked the dark
As much as me.
I hoped
Once I showed you my scars
You would be content here in my collection of shadows.
I remember
How you looked at me so hard
As though you knew
I could only do this once.
Your eyes
Never more alive
Never more willing to see my own.
I felt you look inside of me.
For the first time
I had to be the one to look away.
Exposed
My demons trembled
My flesh
Electric to your touch
In my dark
You never knew who you're holding.
Still you managed
To love us both.

At My Alter

I envy those who know faith
The warmth of the spirit
A holy trinity
That will not fit my angles

My mind has been designed to think far too much
Overpowering the strength of the heart
Where the fire of belief is ignited

Always, in His love I am brought to tears
Compelled by compassion, empathy
For the one who's wrath I've been conditioned to fear

In the hands of man He has been made weapon
A scale of judgment far too harsh for these troubled times
In a world desperate for forgiveness
We know no sanctuary
As though the door has been locked against us in vengeance
And not by the hands of humble humans
Who resist our changing ways.

I exist only to touch the lives I've been blessed to encounter
With kindness, light, love
Still, they would stand to watch me burn
At the side of the one He could not forgive

Cast out to create the alter of our suffering
While laying claim to the creation of our temptation

I believe with every particle of my spirit
In the act of forgiveness
I could never send another
To die for my sins

Home

Would you sing to me a lullaby
 Of the land I used to know?
 Would you whisper me the poetry
 To carry me back home?

Would you hold me close and kiss me hard
 Help me to forget?
 Remind me with a gentle touch
 It gets better yet?

I need to know the day will break
 Over this forever dark.
 I need to know you'll bear the weight
 Of this heavy heart.

I cry for all my fields of green
 For low mountains and my sea
 I need you now to help me somehow
 Bring her back to me.

Wolf Born

Seeking the urge to run deep into the wild night
 To meet the dawn among the brambles and boughs
 To live by the light of the moon
 Stealing sustenance from her silver

My shadow, my comrade
 Sharing the same vigilante mind
 It is a hunt for justice
 For a forest that welcomes
 And trees that dance to my song

I will not be broken nor made to abide in a society of
sheep
Dancing in the face of my blood lust
Thinking their safe pasture
Will tame me

Fault Lines

She never asked for anything, went without
Foolishly believing
Her pain was visible
That though she was in desperate need
She was denied
As she was unworthy.

The fault first lies
In her faith
That all hearts were like her own
Able to recognize the pain
That comes with mere existence
Within a world
Prone to greed & aspirations
Enough to make the gods tremble

Kindred spirits seldom come together
As the world is threatened by their hope
She felt hers waning
A full moon lost
Behind chem trails & excess

Numb was never the answer
And sometimes
The cure hurts more
Than the disease

Shutting down kept her breathing
Yet you could never mistake it for life.

An Ode to Fairy Godmothers

It's a sin we've been sold a lie.
The tragedy is that we fell for it.
Fairytales as scripture
Repenting our sins to wicked stepmothers
While our sisters hold us down.
What star do you wish upon
That would allow you to control the heart of another?
If your definition of Prince Charming
Leaves no room for the hunter and the beast
How will you survive when the glass slipper shatters
Throwing shards deep into your heart?
If you think you've found him,
Forgive me for calling out your devil in disguise.

There is truth amongst the lies
The forest is dark and deep and castles house real
dungeons,
But we are the ones who give birth to the monsters
No one is immune.
The apple was poisoned and we knew it
Still, we bit...
Hungry, deep in a part of ourselves we deny
Begging innocence when we find ourselves
Cramped & sweating with no kiss sweet enough to
curb the pain

We are stone tablets engraved with the sins of our
mothers
Who only wanted better
When they told us we could have anything we
wanted

While clearly pointing out our place
Somewhere between the truth and the lie
With a wave of a magic wand
Our faith in ourselves
Ensnared in illusions of perfection
We have no hope of living up to

Alabaster Disaster

It seems it's the usual order
Coffee & nicotine
Vices I can't quite shake
Reminding me just how human I am

Constant failings in a sea of struggle
Shaking off contentment
...it makes me uncomfortable
...paranoid

Ice storms my window
Our trade off for warmer temperatures
My own little drummer boy
Drowning out the songs I don't want to hear

The dog, curled up on my lap
Could care less about the weather
Much less about the alabaster disaster
He rests his head upon

A porcelain keepsake
Traps the ashes
I've never been the coaster type
Unless you count the way I coast through life

I am not fond of complication
Am prepared to die alone
Yet still
I see eyes in the smoke

That curls round the room

See my future in the grounds
Sticking to the side of my mug
Evil truths
I'm not yet prepared to face
So in disgrace

I light another cigarette
And turn the music up.

Sink

I want to pull you under. Drag you down into the pit of my despair. Perhaps then you'll see this heart you toy with for what it is.

I want to show you everything. The blackness, the sadness. You must know by now this water was born from tears. These waves that threaten,grow stronger because I insist on putting limits on my ocean, still they rage. They have no where else to go.

You feign sympathy. Offer a tissue and proceed to burden me with your own pain. I swallow it all, stifling the screaming as your hurt pours itself to my insides. These depth are not shallow. This rage is not poetry.

My tongue is bleeding from your bite. Your kiss like arsenic, my throat burns, expands. Your body smothering, your scent inhaled rips fire through my insides.

This is not passion. This is not love. This is not so much as infatuation.

This is the story of a girl who had to find a new weapon of choice when they took away her razor.

This is a chapter in a tale that's been told a thousand times and still you can't see how it ends.

That you think I've kept my head above water tells me I've found another who will never hear my cries. Tells me I can send out my distress call over and over again without any fear of being saved.

When that fatal point is finally reached, no one will be able to say I haven't tried.

Christ knows, the world is watching.

Will you be so kind as to at least stand on the sands of my final resting place? When my body, broken and depleted, washes to shore, will you at least look on in wonder, confess your indifference and whisper...

"Who knew?"

Third Trimester

Fire in the Sky

The moment is an ironic one.
Rushing, scambling
To see a building go up in flames

Around the corner
Then gushing
Arrival imminent

Fear takes hold
As the sky breathes flames

He is waiting
Suitcase, car seat
On the front step

Of a tiny gingerbread house
A starter's nest
He will never want to leave.

She feels safe
Suddenly
Knowing her strength is what is needed

When she sees the shine of fear
In the eyes of the soon to be father
As they rush toward the big city
Blood pressure high
Awaiting life on stand by
The lights

Hold them ensnared.

Decisions

They expect you to know so much
Even though you don't know yourself

Career, lifestyle, love
All figured out before you've even started living.

You fall for it all.
The big beautiful lie...

Because if you follow their instructions
You should never have to struggle.

And for a short while, you are fooled
Because life in the beginning is easy

You convince yourself
You are worthy for replication

Worthy enough to guide another

It's life itself that doesn't play along,
While it pleads its innocence.

Though your plan may not change...
People do...you do.

The decisions made at twenty
Are not the same as the ones made at forty

Priorities change
Love alters

Scars make for tougher skin
But the tears are still wet and warm.

Amber

We are fossilized
 Trapped in a timeless existence
 All I ever wanted
 Just within my reach

Immortalized
 Yet my feet are held in place
 Swallowed by a honey tide
 Stuck fast

Immobilized
 Reaching hands to grasp
 Clawing at the cruelness
 Of unfulfilled desire

Demoralized
 Drowning as I clasp
 At something that never was
 Solid enough to hold on to

You escaped the amber
 Left to wonder free
 Yet you choose to linger
 Watch as it takes me

Panic

Space is an illusion
Escape futile
Red has never held the promise of hope
Scarlet letters painted to keep the lie alive

We are dreams within nightmares
Belonging to the monsters we ignore
Ignorance colors our windows
A landscape without form

There is concrete above and below
Every secret wish, hidden longing
Cementing our failures in a world
That would never let us achieve

It remains content to let us keep running
Corner to corner
Locked doors
In a room with an imagined view.

Stray

You have poured yourself into me. Saturating starved limbs
Intoxicating this simple mind.

I am overwhelmed by the flood.
Drunk on excess
Fueled by a craving
Ancient, foreign

I had but withered to dust
Waiting as sacrifice
For the next wind
Ready to let go
Blown like so much ash
Minuscule me

You brought me sustenance
Put meat on my bones
Almost convinced me
I should stay

Then you went away
To watch me wither from a distance

Washing your hands of me
Too much fire, too much sting.

Leaving me to burn alive
No you, to quench my thirst

Rats

There is no room to breathe here
Claustrophobic mindset
But there are mice...then there are rats
I know the difference
By the girth of their tails
In their scramble for the cheese

The darkness hides his contours
But not his scent
A rodent army bows
Not realizing how unsustainable
His kingdom has become

The air stings my lungs
A bitter stench
Stomach bile and Parmesan
I feel their feet
Their tails
Their over fed underbellies warm
As they drag themselves over my chilled flesh

I have never feared death
Could care less who calls my carcass home
But I refuse to confuse
The rats with stars
The shine in their eyes
All knowing

Tigress

I'm being eaten alive by our resources
A hungry tiger
Forever chasing her tail
Hunting balance
Dizzy from the lack of consistency
In my pounce

My roar has been muffled
In a stream of consciousness I have been denying
I know my strength
What I am capable of
I have been that beast

Anger simmers below the surface
The urge to steal silently through the wilds
Fading
The queen of this jungle cannot rule quietly

With knowledge comes power
False confidence
Like a rush of blood to my head
I feel the need
An addict's worst nightmare

Taken down in the chase.

Thru Infinity

Infinity
A fascinating concept
I ponder often

I feel I've known you for it
...and beyond

As though I could share every drugstore romance
Whispered in your ear
While sipping cherry coke through a candy striped
bendy straw
Your hand like a claw
On my thigh on a Friday night in July

Whether its caviar and ice wine
Or laying on a flatbed behind the ballpark bleachers
A downtown high rise
It's still the same stars, the same sky

Do you see this moon tonight?
Pregnant and ripe
Filled with promise?

Tomorrow though,
Same stars, same sky
she will begin to show her waning side

We flow like that, you know
I've been scared of your distance
Only to end up smothered by your presence

I've come to depend on it
I love you so much deeper when you're distant
Hate you hard
Over pizza and beer.

Still you are here
Always and forever
Always am, always will be

Stories written
Through Infinity.

A Celebration Song

She desired much more than what normal would entail.
Her dreams were not of ladders.
She dreaded placing a heavy foot upon the heads that
made the rungs she was to climb.
Still...somewhere inside...
she had reached the sad conclusion,
that if she could make them smile with her actions,
somehow, her soul would be left alone.

Backbone

If I raise this child
With kindness & forgiveness
As the tenements of her existence

Will she be too soft
Like me?

How does one obtain balance
In a world view
Ruled by ego
And the survival of self?

What will I ask her to sacrifice
If I ask her to put others first
Knowing
The good deeds
Will seldom be returned?

I Wonder...

Is there comfort
Found in the voice of a stranger
Or is the reward
Found in the thrill
Of the risk?

Not an Option

The world has proven difficult at best. I fear I am much too weak to continue on. I second guess my decisions on the hour, knowing true happiness leaves no room for doubt.

I have placed cumbersome responsibilities upon my shoulders, and have sought to blame others for the consequences.

These things were never asked of me. Honestly…

My good deeds have been performed with the most selfish of intentions. Call it hope in the afterlife, call it seeking reward. They have been done because my heart was too weak to bear the burden of not doing.

It is the same weight that keeps me here. Trapped in disgusting self-pity and cowardice. I wish not to be responsible for my own happiness. I realize now, I chose this life, so I wouldn't have to be.

I have surrounded myself with the love of good people, family, a few friends I could count on one hand. They love me…and most importantly, they tolerate my half-assed ambitions and day dreams. I figure, if you can find the same, you'll somehow make it through…but they're not you.

Never doubt, I exist because I want that that I cannot have.

It is the hunger that keeps me here.

If I was to accept the sustenance...only having known hunger...I could not promise I could remain.

Too Easy to Love

I am tired of being a victim of circumstance.
I am tired of not knowing forgiveness
When I have so much to give.

Second and third chances
Fourth if they are required
Making those who will never understand
Angry

They love me
Because they have to
A guilt trip
I never intended.

Bury Me

Who do I want to be today?
Opportunities fly at me from every direction.
I wish I could make you understand the strength it takes
not to duck.
To not run back to my bed
Pull the covers over my head
And fall back to the dream.

I'm wise enough to know
It will never come true.
Your wise enough to know
The safety that comes with that.
If I can keep you there on the fringes,
Painted in shadows & stardust
Perhaps I can stave off the disappointment.
Pretend I know what I'm doing.

There's so much I want
That I will never have.
I accept the truth.
Wanting breeds desire
Desire is the breath of life.

I will reach up and grasp this opportunity.
The one that will fill the void with dollars.
Erase time from my agenda
So perhaps my thoughts and my words will cease.

I would be a fool to hide.
To not lend length upon length
To this stretching to make ends meet.

I know money can't buy happiness.
But it can buy you ways to help you forget your misery.
I'll still have the hours between midnight & dawn
To bleed to the page
Cry between the lines
And hide if I have to.

I'll bury the real me there.
It's a dark she knows all too well.

Frailty

He fondles me with flattery. Violating sacred spaces with lyrical words stolen from the greats. Like a poor, lost puppy, I nip at his heels, waiting for language treated as dinner scraps. It is blasphemy, the sweetest sin. A crime against the secret coven who knows not where I stray.

He teases me with poetry. Delectable sonnets that sing of another's beauty, another who's pure of heart. Is it wrong to imagine myself like this? I am no better than those who primp and prep. Those who mutilate themselves on the outside, hoping to catch a stranger's eye. Am I any different because I hope to ensnare a mind?

I have no hope to write of love. It is far too grand a concept for me to fathom. I know what it's not. I know its poetry has been misunderstood. I have knelt before the saints, tears overwhelming me, felt their warmth wash over me. This is the closet I can come to love. I am blessed to know this much. He would have me believe in the parlour tricks, the nakedness, perhaps this is why he cannot write the words himself.

Still, I follow. Hating myself for my vanity. Despising the shallow pangs that come with inattention. Fragile, eggshell self-esteem. One minute soaring, only to be crushed under the weight of this strangely poetic indifference.

The sisters would punish me for this frailty. For confessing my ego needs tended. There is only so much good that comes with burning undergarments. And no good can come from mimicking the monsters they hope to defeat.

I desire only the words. Ears to listen. Lips to share. If they desire to linger elsewhere, it is because at heart I am human. The strongest can only survive solitude for so long.

Put This to Memory

I want to tell you it will be easy.
I want you to believe
That if you work hard enough
Long enough
You will be rightly rewarded
For your effort...

This was the first lie
I had to memorize

I want to tell you to be kind
Above all else
Because kindness begets kindness
And no good deed goes unnoticed

This too
Had to be put to memory
It is no doubt the biggest crock of shit
And will do you the most harm

Most of all
I wish I could tell you
Our law is just
And stands on the side of right

But right does not mean legal
And ethics is the first thing to get tossed
On the psych assessment
Of the brutal enforcers

For the laws as they are written

Must be upheld
Lest our society expose its weakness
And starts to care too much.

The only thing that matters
Is you are on your own
Love while you can
Laugh every chance you get
And never let them break you

We need you
More than you've yet to realize
In spite of every wrong
That will be done against you
Every hurt that is undeserved
You only win
By not letting them.

She Will Not Mourn

She will not mourn this empty bed.
For how can her lover be truly free
if he lies tangled in her sands?

She will not mourn these empty spaces.
Delicate mounds reveal themselves,
awakening, anxious for his return.

Under the spell of the universe
Two bodies
One born of earth to receive
One born of moon to deliver

They fill these empty spaces
for law demands they must
thoughts of the other
magnetizing
drawn and pulled
for they know
without one
purpose disappears for the other.

She will not mourn these scars
Divine flesh, torn
ravaged, consumed by his force

It is in his absence she heals,
preparing for his sure and certain return.
There is no mystery
Only need.

It is the price she pays.
Her blood stays with him,
running, running, running,
through mountains, underground

Until filtered, and his need returns.
His path, lit by the moon
to enter her once again,
driven, power, force

She will not mourn this empty bed
She will not mourn these empty spaces.
She can hear him coming,

Calling,
A fire lit from within
Pulsing,
A thirst only his waters can sate.

How High a Cost

It is an infuriating, maddening and most mundane
conundrum
This sense of entitlement
Where the fine line between self-worth and ego
is near invisible.

We can lose ourselves to selfishness
Somehow believe we deserve more than the next guy
because we've hurt more than the next guy.

I think it's safe to say, there's not anybody here
who isn't hurting.

Chasing the dreams bestowed upon us
by a system as plastic as the currency it's running.
We bow to a faceless megalomaniac
whose stench has destroyed our planet
and forfeited our children's future.
A beast that eats hope
to feed insatiable appetites for control.

And we run,
from one hungry soul to the next
taking more than we give
all in an effort to maintain ourselves.
We consume
grow bored
grow fat
grow lazy
Believing in the holy power of more.
Feeding the holes

with make-believe memories
of times that never were.

Fabricating relationships
on the thinnest of possible threads
We turn away from the truth
because it comes at a price
nearly none of us are willing to pay.

Rape Culture

He stood beside me as the news played on.
I had known him for years
Well meaning, kind hearted, intelligent, educated
White collar to the nines
worked for the government
complete with 1.5 daughters at home
just coming of age in this messed up digital era

Yet again, our hearts both devastated
as news of another young girl
raped, assaulted, and mocked,
by a school, by a community,
by the same digital era that as parents, we both feared
had finally given in to the abuse
and taken her own life.

Four boys, a smart phone camera
yet, despite being the victim
It was she who was shamed.

I watched his face grow whiter
I saw the fear in his eyes
I knew he was thinking of his girls
It gave me hope
until he spoke...

"How are we going to teach our daughters they can't be
getting drunk like that?"

Biting my tongue did no good
the pain was too much to bare...

"How about teaching our sons that just because she's
drunk doesn't mean she wants to fuck"

Crass...perhaps
but how much longer can we deny the issue.

He didn't respond,
and I realized...that same mind, probably didn't think
much of me
being a woman and speaking in such a manner.

The screen shot changed
A flyer on a telephone pole
on the victim's street
bold yellow paper
bold black print

"Support our boys"

My stomach rolled again...
it's been rolling ever since...

Shame on us.

Thrill Alone

A stolen moment...captured on the banks of the lake
where we were never wanted.
They have no idea of the path beaten through the
brambles by feet unworthy.
So close once to being there with papers...formal
ownership
when we believed such things existed.

How is it possible to divide the invincible? There was a
time I never thought it was.
Like the seasons...like warranty deeds
everything changes hands eventually...why would I
assume
we were somehow different...immune to the genocide
born within out hearts.

Wonder if they know how often we slipped into their
drink naked, contamination under a full moon
Trespassing upon lands brought forth by our mother,
stolen by our father, and sold
traded for paper and status, now fenced, like so many
bleeding hearts
trapped in the fear of being alone.

You can feel her dying. Each year, she slips away a little
more sacrificed in the name of progress
This year I will miss her. The moments. The sunsets.
and those illicit memories, drifting away, like the smoke
that fueled our courage

I can smell Spring now, despite the snow and ice that
still decorate the banks
but the brambles remain dead, late blooms hardly
visible
the thrill is not nearly the same alone.
There is no fear of leaving footprints in the snow...no
adrenalin rush from fear of being caught

Knowing I'll not return, I want to holler...stamp my feet
in the treacherous March mud
and scream how dare you.

Yet...it's only my own heart, that knows why

Afterbirth

A strange calm came lingering as the placenta let go. The canal folding back in upon itself, its route, no longer needed, casting off the bloody remains, the circle completed.

The bright light that surrounded her was not the way to heaven. It was the smiling faces of family that surrounded her, now, one stronger in number.

The precious bundle was passed through generations, through bloodlines, as though an ancient and ritualistic baptism was taking place within the sterile confines of the room they would never be able to make feel like home.

Her blue eyes alert, no cries came from the youngest warrior.

Mother looked upon her in awe, proud, humble. She understood now, her fear had been unwarranted. That no matter the road her daughter would set out upon, the hope for better rested within her.

Trial and tribulation, joy and love, all indispensable to building a life worth living. One, without the other, would leave only numb. It was the courage to face and accept both the good and the bad, that Mother would hope to instill. The courage to cry with all her might, to love with all her heart, to feel and to live as we have all been gifted.

As piles of gifts and flowers grew around them, mother
and daughter connected, and the first melodic cry
sounded from the babe.

She was hungry.
Mother did what came to her naturally.
Providing what was needed.
In her breast, her heart swelled.

This, is what mothers were born to do.

Printed in Great Britain
by Amazon